How Cooking Works

DK Publishing

DK

LONDON, NEW YORK, MUNICH,
MELBOURNE, and DELHI

Senior editor Carrie Love
Senior art editor Gemma Fletcher
Designer Lauren Rosier

Photographer Dave King
Home economist Kate Blinman
Science consultant Donald R. Franceschetti
US editor Margaret Parrish
Production editor Siu Chan
Production controller Kara Wallace
Jacket designer Gemma Fletcher
Publishing manager Bridget Giles
Creative director Jane Bull
Category publisher Mary Ling

First published in the United States in 2012
by DK Publishing,
375 Hudson Street
New York, New York 10014

12 13 14 15 16   10 9 8 7 6 5 4 3 2 1
001—182774—02/12

A catalog record for this book
is available from the Library of Congress.
ISBN: 978-0-7566-9004-5

Printed and bound in China
by Hung Hing

Discover more at
www.dk.com

Contents

4 Introduction

6 Tools of the trade

START THE DAY

8 How to cook eggs

10 Pancakes

12 French toast

14 Fruity granola

16 Granola breakfast bars

18 Fruit smoothies

SUPER SNACKS

20 Pea and mint soup

22 Cookie dough

This is fun!

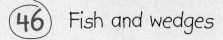

(24) Shrimp skewers

(26) Rice balls

(28) Hummus and popcorn

(30) Salads

MAIN MEALS

(32) Pizza dough

(34) Pizza toppings

(36) Vegetarian moussaka

(38) Lamb hot pot

(40) Mini-burgers

(42) Two pasta dishes

(44) Chili con carne

(46) Fish and wedges

(48) Marinated lime chicken

SWEET STUFF

(50) Blueberry muffins

(52) Strawberry cake

(54) Fruity meringues

(56) Lemon and lime cake

(58) Ice cream

(60) Raspberry crème brûlée

(62) Refrigerator cake

(64) Index

Which one is your favorite recipe to make?

Introduction

Being able to cook is an important skill in life. It's a fun activity, too. This book will inspire you and give you the confidence to try out new dishes for yourself, your family, and your friends.

You'll find simple recipes, such as how to boil an egg or bake muffins, to more complicated dishes, such as moussaka and meringues. Each recipe is clearly laid out and easy to follow.

So, put on your apron and get cooking!

How this book works

It's important to check carefully the "You will need:" box before you go shopping for the ingredients.

Each recipe has an introduction to inspire and encourage you to try out the dish.

You'll find suggestions for alternative ingredients to try out or extra items of food to accompany a dish.

Keep an eye out for any "Special equipment:" you might need to complete a recipe. Make sure you have everything prepared before you get cooking.

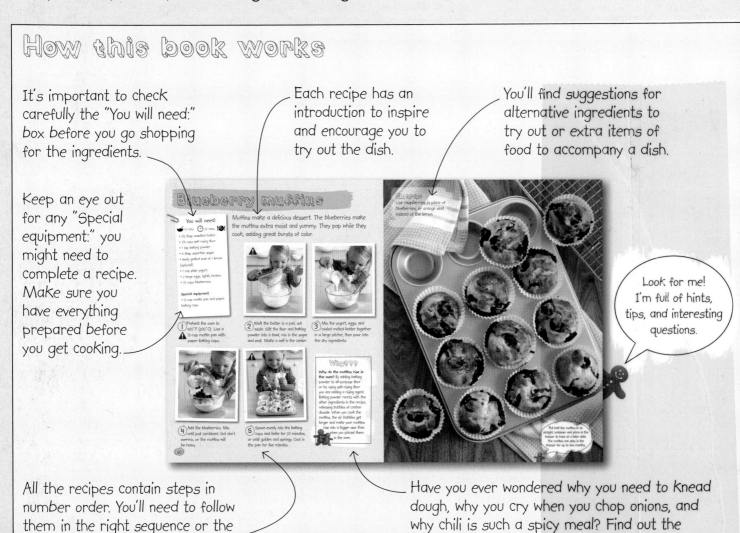

Look for me! I'm full of hints, tips, and interesting questions.

All the recipes contain steps in number order. You'll need to follow them in the right sequence or the recipe won't work.

Have you ever wondered why you need to knead dough, why you cry when you chop onions, and why chili is such a spicy meal? Find out the scientific answers to these questions and more by reading the "Why???" boxes.

Getting started

Roll up your sleeves, wear an apron, tie up long hair, and wash your hands before you start any recipe. Store food correctly and follow expiration dates. Wash all fruit and vegetables before you use them in a recipe. Clean up any spills as you go. Use separate cutting boards to cut up vegetables and meat. Wash your hands after handling raw meat and eggs.

KEY

Key to symbols used in the recipes:

 Check this symbol to find out how long it takes to prepare a recipe.

 This symbol tells you how long it takes to cook a dish.

 This symbol tells you how many servings a recipe makes. Keep in mind that really young children eat less than older children and adults, so a recipe will make more portions for younger children.

 This symbol means that a step requires closer adult supervision, or an adult should carry out the instructions. An adult should always be with a child when making any recipe from this book.

WEIGHTS AND MEASUREMENTS

Make sure you weigh the ingredients correctly. Use measuring spoons, a measuring cup, and weighing scales, where necessary. Measurements are written out in full below. You'll see the abbreviations in the "You will need:" boxes.

Metric measures:	Imperial measures:	Spoon measures:
g = grams	oz = ounces	tsp = teaspoon
ml = milliliters	lb = pounds	tbsp = tablespoon
	fl oz = fluid ounces	

A wooden spoon is a cook's friend. I'm used in lots of recipes.

Tools of the trade

It's important that you use the right equipment for each recipe. Most kitchens are equipped with the majority of these "tools." Remember to be careful around equipment that is sharp or uses electricity to power it. An adult should always supervise you while you're in the kitchen.

Peelers

Garlic crusher

Wooden spoons

Whisk

Basting brush

Kitchen scissors

Large spoon

Pizza cutter

Sharp Knife

Table Knife

Fork

Spoons

Grater

Baking sheets

Loaf pan

Muffin pan

Pizza tray

Cutting boards

Small bowls

Large bowl

Colander

Glass bowls

Get the equipment ready before you start a recipe.

Cutting board

Food processor

Glass jar

Masher

Electric mixer

Spatula

Plastic spatula

Skewers

Strainer

Blender

Slotted spoon

Spaghetti claw

Did you know the bottom of a springform pan comes out?

Measuring cup

Square cake pan

Ramekin

Lemon juicer

Springform cake pan

Glass pitchers

Rolling pin

Baking dish

Cooling rack

Parchment paper

Frying pan

Saucepan with lid

Saucepans in different sizes

Stock pot

Milk pan

Do you have all of these tools in your kitchen?

How to cook eggs

Eggs are perfect for breakfast, since they're packed with goodness to start your day. You can try cooking eggs in different ways to vary your breakfast.

Scrambled eggs with bacon

1. Ask an adult to broil the bacon. When it's cooked, use a knife and fork to cut it up into small pieces.

2. Whisk together the milk and egg, until creamy.

You can use brown or white toasted bread.

Serve the scrambled egg and bacon on toast, with basil sprinkled on top.

3. Melt the butter in a frying pan over medium heat and add the egg and milk mixture. Stir often until the eggs are just cooked, but still creamy. Mix in the broiled bacon pieces.

Boiled eggs

You will need:
🥣 2 mins   ⏰ 4-8 mins 🍴

- 1 egg
- 1 piece of buttered toast, sliced

How do you like your egg boiled? Look at the options below and decide how long to cook your egg. Fill a small saucepan with water and lower one egg into it. Ask an adult to boil the water. When the water has boiled, lower the temperature and let it simmer.

SOFT-BOILED
Cook for four minutes. This egg will have a soft, runny yolk—perfect for dipping your slices of toast into!

MEDIUM-BOILED
Cook for six minutes. The egg yolk will be medium-firm.

HARD-BOILED
Cook for eight minutes. The yolk will be really firm.

Fried eggs

You will need:
🥣 1 min   ⏰ 2-4 mins 🍴

- 1 tsp sunflower oil
- 1 egg
- 1 slice of buttered toast
- ground black pepper, to season

1. Ask an adult to heat the oil in a pan over medium heat.

2. Crack the egg into a bowl. If any of the shell falls into the bowl, scoop it out using a spoon. Gently pour the egg into the frying pan.

3. The egg needs to be fried for about two minutes over medium heat. If you like your egg well-done, it needs to be cooked on both sides.

4. Serve the fried egg on a slice of toast. Season with black pepper.

Pancakes

Pancakes can be thick or thin, depending on the ingredients you use to make them. Have fun trying out both types of pancake. Thin pancakes are called "crêpes." Make this dish for your family.

Thick pancakes

You will need:

 5 mins 12-15 mins 4

- 1 egg
- 1 cup less 1 tbsp self-rising flour
- 1 tsp baking soda
- 2/3 cup milk
- sunflower oil for frying
- 7oz (200g) fresh strawberries, hulled and sliced
- 4 tbsp plain yogurt

1. Put the egg, flour, baking soda, and milk into a bowl. Whisk up the mixture until it's smooth.

2. Ask an adult to heat a tablespoon of sunflower oil in a frying pan. Use a large spoon to pour the pancake mixture carefully into the pan.

Crêpes

To make crêpes, you need to mix together the following ingredients and cook the mixture in a nonstick frying pan over medium heat.

You will need:

 5 mins 10 mins 3

- 1 cup all-purpose flour
- 1 large egg
- 1¼ cups milk
- serve with 1 sliced banana and chocolate sauce or lemon juice and sugar

Can you flip your crêpe over? Be careful!

3. Fry the pancake until it is golden brown on the bottom and bubbling on the top. Flip the pancake over and fry it on the other side until golden brown.

4 Serve your pancakes with strawberries and plain yogurt.

Try out other berries on your pancakes.

Why???

Why are thick pancakes full of air bubbles? Baking powder and baking soda act as rising agents. They react with the other ingredients and release a gas called carbon dioxide that causes the batter to rise and fill with *bubbles*.

You will need:

🥣 6 mins   🕐 10 mins   🍴❹

- 4 large eggs
- 1 cup milk
- ¼ tsp ground cinnamon
- 4 slices thick white bread, cut into triangles
- 2 tbsp sunflower oil
- ⅔ cup blueberries
- maple syrup, to serve

It may be called French toast, but this dish is popular around the world. In Spain and Brazil, it's an Easter dessert; in Portugal, it's eaten at Christmastime. French toast can be eaten as a savory or sweet meal. Try making it for your family.

(1) Crack the eggs into a mixing bowl. Add the milk and cinnamon and whisk together.

(2) Pour the mixture into a shallow dish. Soak the bread triangles in the mixture. Only soak the triangles for 20 seconds on each side, since you don't want them to get too soggy!

Which topping do you like best?

(3) Heat half a tablespoon of the oil in a frying pan on low heat. Carefully place two triangles in the pan.

(4) Fry the triangles on both sides until they turn golden. Repeat steps 3 and 4 for the remaining triangles.

(5) Serve the French toast with blueberries and maple syrup or try it with butter and jam.

Why use oil for frying? The hot sunflower oil stops the French toast from sticking to the pan while it's being fried. The oil reduces friction with the pan. Don't let the pan get too hot or the bread will burn!

Fruity granola

You need a hearty breakfast to keep you going through the morning. This recipe will keep you filled up until lunchtime.

You will need:

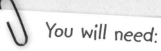 5 mins · 20 mins · 8

- 2 tbsp sunflower oil
- 6 tbsp light corn syrup or honey
- 3 cups rolled oats
- 1 cup hazelnuts
- ½ cup pumpkin seeds
- ⅔ cup dried banana chips, broken into small pieces
- ⅔ cup raisins
- milk or plain yogurt, to serve

1. Ask an adult to preheat the oven to 400°F (200°C). Melt the oil and corn syrup or honey in a saucepan over low heat.

2. Pour the syrup and oil mixture into a large bowl with the oats, hazelnuts, and pumpkin seeds.

Try using other dried fruits, such as apricots.

Why???

Why does the granola turn golden brown when it's baked? When the granola is baked in an oven at a high temperature the sugar in it reacts to the heat and caramelizes, turning the outside edges to a yummy golden brown color.

3. Place the mixture onto a baking sheet, spread it out, and cook in the oven for 10 minutes, or until the granola turns a golden brown color.

4. Let the oat mixture cool down and then pour it into a bowl. Add the dried banana chips and raisins to the mixture and stir well.

Store your granola in an airtight container and have it for breakfast a few times over a couple of weeks. Don't keep it to yourself! Let your family and friends try it, too.

5 Serve your granola in a bowl with milk or a spoonful of plain yogurt.

Granola breakfast bars

Granola bars are perfect for breakfast or as a snack later on in the day. Once you've mastered this recipe, you can try it out using other dried fruit and nuts. This recipe makes 12 yummy bars.

 Make sure the nuts are chopped well.

You will need:

 15 mins   30 mins   12

- ½ cup unsalted butter
- ½ cup less 2 tbsp light brown sugar
- ⅓ cup light corn syrup or honey
- 2½ cups rolled oats
- ½ cup raisins
- ½ cup mixed nuts, chopped

Special equipment: 12 x 9 x 1½in (30 x 23 x 4cm) baking pan

⚠ **1** Ask an adult to preheat the oven to 300°F (150°C) and grease your baking pan.

2 Ask an adult to melt the butter, sugar, and corn syrup (or honey) in a saucepan over low heat.

3 Mix together the melted ingredients with the rest of the ingredients in a large bowl.

A masher is useful for flattening the mixture.

Why???

Why do the ingredients stick together? The sugar and corn syrup act like a glue in this recipe. They help the dry ingredients to stick together, making the granola bars incredibly chewy and sticky!

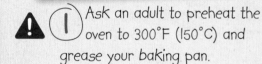

4 Spread the mixture evenly in the baking pan. Bake for 20–30 minutes (or until golden brown).

5 When the granola bars are baked, cut them into 12 squares. Hold the warm pan with a cloth. Take the squares out when they're cold.

Fruit smoothies

Smoothies are fun to make and drink! You can create lots of variations by using different fruit or by adding rolled oats to make your drink a bit thicker.

You will need:

🥣 7 mins 🍴 3

- ½ cup pulp-free orange juice
- ½ cup milk
- ½ cup plain yogurt
- 1 cup blueberries
- 1 cup strawberries, hulled
- 3 tbsp rolled oats
- ½ tsp vanilla extract (optional)

Special equipment
- blender

Blueberry, orange, and strawberry smoothie

If your smoothie is too thick you can add water.

Don't forget to put the lid on the blender!

Drink right away or you'll need to stir your smoothie, since it will thicken and can separate.

1. Put all the ingredients into a blender and run it on medium to high speed until everything is well mixed and smooth.

2. Pour the smoothie into three glasses and serve it to your family or friends.

🥣 7 mins 🍴③

For the banana and mango smoothie:

- ¾ cup milk
- ½ cup plain yogurt
- 2 small bananas, sliced
- 1 small mango, peeled and roughly chopped

🥣 7 mins 🍴③

For the peach and berry smoothie:

- ½ cup milk
- ½ cup plain yogurt
- 2 peaches, sliced
- ½ cup raspberries
- ½ cup strawberries, hulled
- 1 tbsp rolled oats

After you've tried these smoothies, you can make up one of your own! Experiment with different flavors and textures.

Banana and mango smoothie

Peach and berry smoothie

Why???

Why do fruit smoothies taste so sweet? Fruit is high in natural sugars, so when mixed with yogurt and milk it adds natural sweetness. The smoothies will be sweeter if you use ripe fruit.

Why do smoothies have bubbles in the drink and on the surface? When you process the smoothie in a blender it mixes air with the ingredients, forming tiny air bubbles throughout the drink.

Pea and mint soup

You will need:

 10 mins   🕐 5 mins   🍴🍽️④

- 2¼ cups frozen peas, such as petit pois
- 2 cups vegetable stock
- pinch of freshly grated nutmeg
- handful of fresh mint leaves, roughly chopped, or 1 tbsp of dried mint
- a few fresh thyme stalks, leaves picked (optional)
- ground black pepper
- 4 slices of crusty bread, to serve

Special equipment
- electric blender

This soup can be eaten hot or cold, so you can have it all year round! For a different flavor you can add bacon and heavy cream.

Either heat it in a pan or chill it in the refrigerator.

① Put the peas in a bowl, then pour boiling water over them, cover, and leave to stand for about five minutes. Pour into a colander over the sink to drain off the water.

② Using a blender, process the peas, stock, nutmeg, and herbs until smooth and combined. Add more stock if the soup is too thick. Season well with black pepper.

Extras

You can add one tablespoon of sour or heavy cream to each portion of soup to make it nice and creamy. If you like bacon, then ask an adult to broil four slices. Cut up a slice for each cup of soup. The combination is delicious!

Why???

Why can this soup be eaten hot or cold? Most dishes need to be served either hot or cold, but this soup can be eaten either way. Since the peas are cooked in the hot water in the first step, they can be cooled down to eat or heated up.

Cookie dough

You will need:

🥣 10 mins ⏱ 15 mins 🍽 15

SWEET DOUGH

- ½ cup butter, at room temperature
- 1 egg
- ½ cup superfine sugar
- ½ tsp vanilla extract
- 1½ cups self-rising flour

SAVORY DOUGH

- ½ cup butter, at room temperature
- 1 egg
- 1½ cups self-rising flour

Special equipment:

- electric hand mixer

First, decide whether to make sweet or savory dough. Then choose the extra yummy ingredients you'll add.

⚠ ① Preheat the oven to 350°F (180°C). Line two baking sheets with parchment paper.

② In a bowl, use an electric mixer to beat the butter and egg together (add the sugar and vanilla if you're making a sweet dough).

③ Work in the flour with a spoon until the mixture forms a soft dough, then mix in your additional ingredients (see below).

④ Roll the dough into about 15 balls and place on the baking sheets, leaving space around each ball. Flatten the balls slightly and bake in the oven for 15 minutes, or until golden.

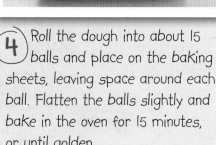

Transfer the cookies to a wire rack to cool.

Cookie variations
Now, choose from the following options.

Sweet cookies

Traditional chocolate chip
½ cup dark or milk chocolate chips

Raisin spice
⅓ cup raisins
¼ tsp apple pie spice

Apricots and cinnamon
⅓ cup dried apricots, finely chopped
¼ tsp ground cinnamon

Cocoa and white chocolate
1 tbsp cocoa powder
½ cup white chocolate chips

Savory cookies

Parmesan and pumpkin seed
1¾oz (50g) fresh Parmesan, grated
¼ cup pumpkin seeds
3 tbsp water

Cheddar cheese and rosemary
1¾oz (50g) Cheddar cheese, grated
1 tbsp sesame seeds
1 tbsp fresh rosemary
3 tbsp water

Pesto, tomato, and olive
¼ cup sundried tomatoes, finely chopped
1 tbsp green pesto
1oz (30g) black olives, finely chopped
3 tbsp water

Tomato paste and pine nuts
⅓ cup pine nuts
1 tbsp tomato paste
1 tsp poppy seeds
3 tbsp water

Cheddar cheese and rosemary

Traditional chocolate chip

Raisin spice

Apricots and cinnamon

Parmesan and pumpkin seed

Pesto, tomato, and olive

Tomato paste and pine nuts

Traditional chocolate chip

Cheddar cheese and rosemary

Parmesan and pumpkin seed

Pesto, tomato, and olive

Cocoa and white chocolate

You will need:

🥣 25 mins ⏰ 15 mins 🍴④

For the marinade:
- juice of 1 lemon
- juice of 1 lime
- 2 tbsp soy sauce (reduced salt)
- 1 garlic clove, crushed or finely chopped
- 1 tsp light brown sugar

For the skewers:
- ½ red bell pepper
- ½ yellow bell pepper
- 1 small zucchini
- ½ red onion
- 8 cherry tomatoes
- 5½oz (150g) cooked, peeled jumbo shrimp
- salad, to serve (optional)

Special equipment:
- 4 wooden skewers
- rectangular dish long enough to fit the length of the skewers

Shrimp skewers

Try out this filling and healthy dish. It's fun to create and tastes delicious. If you don't like shrimp, you can use chicken instead.

① Make the marinade by mixing the ingredients together in a pitcher. Carefully cut the bell peppers and red onions into chunks.

② Slice the zucchini.

③ Thread the vegetables and shrimp onto the skewers. Place the skewers into a rectangle dish.

④ Pour the marinade over the skewers. Put the skewers into the refrigerator for an hour. Turn them over after 30 minutes.

⑤ Ask an adult to broil the skewers for 15 minutes. Baste the shrimp every five minutes with the marinade (discard any leftover marinade).

Rice balls

This is a fun and easy snack to make. It also works well as an appetizer before a main meal. The soft rice and melted mozzarella are yummy and have a great texture.

You will need:

 30 mins   5 mins   🍴 4

- 2 cups cold, cooked Arborio or other risotto rice
- ground black pepper
- 1 ball of buffalo mozzarella, cut into cubes
- 1 egg, beaten
- 2 slices of toast, for bread crumbs
- olive oil, for deep-frying
- salsa dip, to serve
- salad, to serve

1. Generously season the rice with black pepper. Roll the rice into 12 even-sized balls.

2. Push a cube of cheese into the center of each ball, then cover so that the cheese is enclosed.

Be extra careful around hot oil. Ask an adult to do the frying.

Why???

Why does mozzarella cheese melt easily? Not all cheeses melt that well. Halloumi and feta, for example, don't lose their shape and flow when they're broiled, fried, or baked, whereas mozzarella changes from a solid to a more stringy, liquid form when it's heated. Mozzarella is the perfect cheese to use for this yummy dish, but you can also try Cheddar cheese.

3. Roll each ball in the egg and then roll in the bread crumbs (toast that's been turned into crumbs in a food processor).

4. Ask an adult to deep-fry the balls in olive oil over medium heat for two to three minutes, or until golden.

Buy a salsa dip to serve with
the rice balls. You can make
this into a light meal by
adding vegetables. Try a fresh
garden salad with leaves,
cherry tomatoes, and
cucumber slices.

Hummus

Hummus is a tasty snack made from chickpeas. Your body needs protein and fiber—chickpeas are high in both!

You will need:

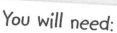  8 mins

- 15.5oz (439g) can chickpeas, drained and rinsed
- 2 garlic cloves, crushed
- juice of 1 lemon, plus extra, if needed
- 2-3 tbsp tahini
- 2-3 tbsp olive oil
- 1 cucumber, cut into short sticks
- 4 carrots, peeled and sliced into sticks
- 3 celery sticks, cut
- pita bread (optional)

Special equipment:
- blender or food processor

1 Put all the ingredients (apart from the oil) into a blender or food processor and blend until smooth.

2 Gradually add the oil, a little at a time, until the hummus reaches a dipping consistency. Taste, and add some extra lemon juice if you like. Blend again.

3 Serve as a dip with cucumber, carrot, and celery sticks. Alternatively, if you want a more filling snack, then serve with slices of pita bread.

Add 1-2 tbsp of water if the hummus is too thick.

Extras

Make the hummus recipe and then add one of the options below. Blend until smooth. They're both delicious alternatives and will add flavor to the hummus.

OPTION 1
- 1½oz (50g) sun-dried tomatoes, drained and rinsed if they come in oil

OPTION 2
- 2½oz (75g) black olives, pitted and rinsed

Popcorn

The smell of popcorn popping will make your mouth water. It's a delicious treat that can be savory or sweet.

You will need:

 1 min    3-4 mins 6

- 1 tbsp sunflower oil
- 3½oz (100g) popcorn kernels

Why???

Why does the corn pop?
When you heat popcorn kernels in oil, the heat makes the moisture in the starchy insides expand as steam. It builds up pressure inside the hard outside skin of the kernel. It eventually explodes and the starch puffs up. The explosion makes a popping sound.

1) Pour the kernels and oil into a saucepan. Make sure the lid is secure. Ask an adult to heat the pan on the stove.

2) Let the popcorn pop for a minute. Listen for when the popping slows down. Ask an adult to shake the pan. Let the remaining corn pop.

3) Pour the popcorn into two large bowls. Make one savory and one sweet bowl of popcorn by using the options below.

Sweet popcorn

Ask an adult to melt 2 tsp of unsalted butter in a small pan on low heat. Add ¼ tsp ground cinnamon and ½ tbsp of light brown sugar. Stir until everything is well mixed. Slowly pour the mixture into the popcorn, stirring as you go.

Savory popcorn

Ask an adult to melt 1 tbsp of salted butter in a small pan on low heat. Add ½ tsp of paprika and stir until it's mixed in well with the butter. Slowly pour the mixture into the popcorn, stirring as you go.

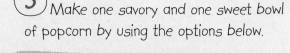

Salads

Salads are good for you, since they help you to get your five portions of fruit and vegetables a day. These super salads are full of interesting ingredients and they're fun to make.

You will need:

 30 mins 🍴4

Tomato and couscous salad:
- 4 large tomatoes
- $2/3$ cup tomato juice
- $3/4$ cup couscous
- $1/3$ cup golden raisins
- handful of basil leaves, chopped
- handful of flat-leaf parsley, torn (optional)
- ground black pepper

Tomato and couscous salad

1 Slice the tops off the tomatoes and scoop out the insides. Put the seeds and flesh into a bowl with the tomato juice.

2 Pour $2/3$ cup of hot water over the couscous and leave to stand for 10 minutes. Fluff up the grains. Add the tomato mixture.

3 Add the golden raisins, basil, and parsley (if using), and mix. Taste, and season with ground black pepper, as needed.

4 Spoon the mixture into the reserved tomato shells. Any leftover couscous can be served on the side.

Try using roasted red bell peppers instead of tomatoes.

Tuna and bean salad

1 Soak the fava beans in hot water for five minutes, then use a colander to drain. Set aside.

2 To make the dressing, put all the ingredients in a screw-top jar, season with black pepper, cover with the lid, and shake!

Tuna and bean salad:
- 1 cup frozen fava beans
- 12oz (340g) cans tuna in olive oil, drained
- 10 cherry tomatoes, halved
- handful of fresh chives, finely chopped
- ground black pepper
- 12 black olives, pitted
- 1 crisp lettuce such as Romaine, leaves separated
- 2-3 scallions, finely sliced

For the dressing you will need:
- 6 tbsp extra virgin olive oil
- 1 garlic clove, finely chopped
- 2 tbsp lemon juice
- 1-2 tsp Dijon mustard

3 Put the tuna, tomatoes, and half of the dressing in a bowl. Sprinkle in half of the chives and season with black pepper. Gently mix in the beans and olives.

4 Spoon the tuna mixture on top of the lettuce. Drizzle with the remaining dressing, and sprinkle the scallions and remaining chives over the top.

Why???

Why do I shake the salad dressing?
The salad dressing is made with oil and lemon juice. Lemon juice is watery. Oil and water do not mix. Shaking the dressing breaks up the oil into small drops that sit in the lemon juice for a while. The mixture separates again if you leave it.

Pizza dough

Invite three friends over for a pizza party at your house. You can have fun making the dough and choosing which toppings to have on your pizza base.

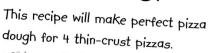

You will need:

60 mins

This recipe will make perfect pizza dough for 4 thin-crust pizzas.

- 3²/₃ cups "00" or strong white flour
- 1/4oz (7g) package instant yeast
- a pinch of salt
- 1¹/₃ cups warm water
- 4 tbsp olive oil

1) Sift the flour into a bowl and add the yeast and salt. Make a well in the center, then slowly add the warm water.

2) Mix with a wooden spoon until it comes together and then add the olive oil and continue to mix until it forms a soft dough.

3) Knead firmly using the heel of your hand, folding the dough over for five minutes until the dough is smooth and stretchy.

4) Put the dough in a bowl, cover with plastic wrap, and leave in a warm place for 30–40 minutes or until the dough has doubled in size.

5) Put the dough out on a floured surface, and knead and fold to punch out the air. Fold the dough over and knead again.

6) Divide the dough into four balls ready to make your pizzas (see pages 34–35 for toppings).

Why do you knead dough?
To create a stretchy dough you need to knead the mixture. This makes the molecules of wheat protein (gluten) in flour get tangled, making the dough stronger. Kneading also helps the yeast to make the dough rise.

Pizza toppings

Now that you've made the dough, choose a pizza topping from these four options. Each person can try one of the recipes, and you can share the end product with your friends.

> Use a floured surface so the dough doesn't stick.

Mozzarella and mushroom

You will need:

🥣 15 mins   🕐 10 mins   🍴 4

- 1 tbsp olive oil
- 4½oz (125g) mushrooms, sliced
- all-purpose flour, for floured surface
- 1 ball of pizza dough per pizza (see pages 32–33)
- 2-3 tbsp tomato paste or puree
- 5½oz (150g) mozzarella, torn into pieces

1) Preheat the oven to 475°F (240°C). Place a tray in the ⚠ oven to get hot.

2) Meanwhile, heat the oil in a pan, add the mushrooms, and fry, stirring, over low heat for two minutes.

3) Roll out the dough on a floured surface. Roll the dough as thinly as you can, rolling away from you and turning it as you go.

4) The pizza base needs to be about 8in (20cm) wide. Spread the tomato sauce over the base and smooth it out evenly.

5) Top with mushrooms, then the cheese. Bake for 10 minutes, until the crust is golden and the cheese is bubbling.

Why???

Why do you shred or grate mozzarella cheese before it goes on the pizza? By grating cheese or shredding it into small pieces, it increases the surface area that's in contact with the heat source. This reduces the amount of time it takes the cheese to melt.

🥣 8 mins 🕙 10 mins 🍴4

For the pepper and pepperoni pizza:

• 2-3 tbsp tomato paste or puree

• 10 small slices of pepperoni

• half a yellow bell pepper, sliced

• 5½oz (150g) mozzarella, torn into pieces

🥣 8 mins 🕙 10 mins 🍴4

For the ham and pineapple pizza:

• 2-3 tbsp tomato paste or puree

• 3 slices of ham, cut into strips

• 1 small can of pineapple pieces, drained

• 5½oz (150g) mozzarella, torn into pieces

Which flavor do you like the best?

Pepper and pepperoni pizza

Ham and pineapple pizza

Mozzarella and mushroom pizza

Tomato and olive pizza

This pizza is made without cheese, but if you really love cheese on your pizza, you can add two handfuls of grated mozzarella before you place the tomatoes and olives.

🥣 8 mins 🕙 10 mins 🍴4

For the tomato and olive pizza:

• 2-3 tbsp tomato paste or puree

• 3 tomatoes, sliced

• handful of pitted black olives, sliced

• fresh basil leaves, to serve

Vegetarian moussaka

Traditional moussaka is made with meat and eggplant, but this vegetarian version is just as good! The pine nuts and cannellini beans give it a fantastic texture.

You will need:

 15 mins   30 mins 6

- 1 tbsp olive oil
- 1 onion, finely chopped
- 1 tsp dried mint
- 3 tsp dried oregano
- 15.5oz (439g) can cannellini beans, drained and rinsed
- 24oz (680g) jar tomato puree or 2 x 14.5oz (411g) cans chopped tomatoes
- 1 cup pine nuts
- 1 cup Greek-style yogurt
- 1 egg
- salad, to serve

Why???

What does it mean "to sweat" an onion?
The technique of sweating food means that you try to make the food release water to soften it without browning. When you sweat an onion you need to keep a lid on the pan so the evaporated water doesn't escape. Keep the burner on low heat and let the onion stew in it's own juice for a while. This will help intensify the flavor.

1 Ask an adult to preheat the oven to 400°F (200°C).

2 Heat the oil in a pan over low heat. Add the onion and sweat gently, until soft. Stir in the mint and one teaspoon of the oregano.

3 Add the cannellini beans, tomato puree, and pine nuts, and bring to a boil. Reduce the heat and simmer gently, until thickened.

4 Spoon the bean mixture into an ovenproof dish.

5 In a new bowl, mix together the yogurt, egg, and remaining oregano. Spoon the yogurt evenly over the top of the bean mixture. Bake in the oven for 15–20 minutes, until the top is golden and set.

You can serve this dish with a side salad.

Lamb hot pot

This hot pot is a hearty main meal that will fill you up. The lamb and tomatoes make it juicy and the chickpeas add texture. Serve it with crusty bread rolls.

1. Put the lamb, flour, and paprika into a mixing bowl and combine well so that the lamb is coated.

2. Heat the oil in a large pan over medium heat, add the onions, and cook, stirring often, for five minutes. Add the lamb and cook until browned.

3. Stir in the garlic and chickpeas, and cook for one minute. Add the tomatoes, bring to a boil, then simmer for 15 minutes.

4. Season well with ground black pepper, stir in the spinach, and cook for three minutes.

Why???

Why do you need to cook meat thoroughly? It's really important to cook meat well before you eat it to kill the bacteria that might multiply enough to cause "food poisoning" before it is eaten. You should also store meat correctly and use it by the expiration date. The best place to thaw frozen meat is in the refrigerator.

Mini-burgers

These mini-burgers are hard to beat. Make them for your family and friends. They'll soon be asking you when you're going to make them again!

You will need:

🥣 30 mins ⏰ 15 mins 🍴 6

For the burgers:
- 9oz (250g) lean ground beef
- 1¾oz (50g) Parmesan cheese, freshly grated
- ½ cup fresh bread crumbs
- 1½ tbsp olive oil
- ½ garlic clove, crushed
- 1 tbsp finely chopped onion
- 1 egg, beaten
- 1 tsp dried oregano
- olive oil, for frying

The recipe makes 12-16 burgers, so you will need the following to serve:
- 12-16 mini bread rolls
- 2 tomatoes, thinly sliced
- lettuce leaves
- 14.5oz (411g) jar of good-quality tomato sauce or salsa

① Mix all the ingredients for the burgers in a bowl. Use your hands to mix everything well.

② Form the mixture into balls about the size of walnuts and then flatten them. Chill the meatballs in the refrigerator. Wash your hands well.

Add slices of Cheddar cheese to make cheese-burgers!

Why???

Why do the bread crumbs help to hold everything together? Bread crumbs are dry and absorb moisture from the meat, helping it to stick together. You make bread crumbs by processing bread in a food processor until it becomes small crumbs.

③ Fry the burgers over medium heat. Make sure the meat is cooked through by putting a fork in and checking that the juice is clear.

④ Carefully cut the rolls in half. Fill each roll with a cooked burger, a tomato slice, a lettuce leaf, and tomato sauce.

You can decorate your mini-burgers before serving them. Make flags out of colored strips of paper.

Two pasta dishes

These pasta dishes make perfect main meals for you and your family. The tomato pasta is deliciously fresh and quick to make and the beef and mushroom pasta is simple and super-tasty.

Pasta with no-cook tomato sauce

You will need:

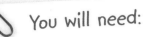 

5 mins   10 mins   4

- 5 tomatoes, deseeded and roughly chopped
- 2 garlic cloves, finely chopped
- handful of basil leaves, torn
- 2 tbsp extra virgin olive oil
- ground black pepper
- 7oz (200g) farfalle pasta
- Parmesan cheese, freshly grated, to serve

Sprinkle Parmesan cheese over the pasta.

1. Put the tomatoes, garlic, basil, and olive oil in a large bowl and season with black pepper. Stir the mixture together.

2. Ask an adult to cook the pasta in a pan of boiling water for 10 minutes. Drain well, then toss with the tomato sauce and serve.

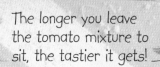

The longer you leave the tomato mixture to sit, the tastier it gets!

42

Pasta with beef and mushroom sauce

You will need:

🥣 10 mins   🕐 25 mins   🍴4

- 1 small onion, finely chopped
- ½ tbsp olive oil
- ground black pepper
- 9oz (250g) lean ground beef
- 3½oz (100g) mushrooms, finely chopped
- pinch of dried oregano
- 1 garlic clove, finely chopped
- 14.5oz (411g) can of chopped tomatoes
- 1 tbsp tomato paste
- 1 tsp green pesto
- 7oz (200g) tortiglioni pasta

1 Cook the onion in the oil over low heat. Season with pepper, then stir in the beef and cook, stirring until no longer pink.

2 Add the mushrooms, oregano, garlic, tomatoes, and tomato paste and stir well. Simmer for 10 minutes, then stir in the pesto.

Tossing pasta with the water it was cooked in helps the sauce to cling better.

3 Meanwhile, ask an adult to cook the pasta in a pan of boiling water. Drain the pasta and toss with the meat sauce and serve.

Why???

Why does pasta get soggy if you overcook it?
When you put hard, uncooked pasta in water and boil it, the pasta becomes soft and grows bigger. The pasta soaks up the water, just like a sponge. If you cook the pasta for too long, it ends up getting soggy because it has absorbed too much water.

You will need:

 30 mins ⏱ 40 mins 🍴6

- 1½ large onions, diced
- 9oz (250g) lean ground beef
- 1 garlic clove, finely chopped
- ½ green chile, finely chopped
- ¼ tsp chili powder
- ¼ tsp paprika
- 15.5oz (439g) can red kidney beans, drained and rinsed
- 1 bay leaf
- 14.5oz (411g) can chopped tomatoes
- ½ tsp dried oregano
- ground black pepper
- basmati rice, to serve

This dish has a kick to it, so if you don't like your food too spicy then you should use less of the chile pepper. You can serve it with tortilla chips, salsa, and guacamole.

Ask an adult to cut up the chile. It can sting your eyes if you get it on your fingers and then touch your eyes.

1) Cook the onions and meat for five minutes. Stir in the garlic, chile, chili powder, and paprika, and cook for five minutes.

2) Add the kidney beans and bay leaf; fry for two minutes.

3) Add the tomatoes and oregano. Bring to a boil, season with pepper, then simmer on low heat for 40 minutes, stirring occasionally.

4) Ask an adult to cook the rice according to the package instructions. Drain using a colander. Take the bay leaf out of the chili.

Why???

Why is this dish so spicy? When you cook with chiles you add a spicy, hot element to your dish. This is because chiles contain capsaicin, the oil that gives them their heat. There are more than 200 types of chile and they vary in size, color, and level of heat.

Why do I cry when I chop onions? Onions contain sulfur chemicals that react with oxygen in the air when cut. The chemicals sting your eyes. Your body produces tears to protect your eyes.

You can serve this dish with tortilla chips. It's fun to dip them in your chili.

Fish and wedges

"Fish and chips" is a traditional British favorite. Try making sweet potato wedges instead of the fries that normally accompany this dish.

 You will need:

 8 mins   25 mins   4

For the sweet potato wedges:
• 2 large sweet potatoes
• 2 tbsp olive oil
• Special equipment: large baking sheet

20 mins   10 mins   4

For the battered fish:
• 1 cup plus 2 tbsp all-purpose flour
• 1 tsp baking soda
• 1 tsp paprika
• ²⁄₃ cup cold soda water
• 1 cup sunflower or corn oil
• 10oz (300g) white fish, such as pollock or cod, cut into ½ in (1cm) strips

Sweet potato wedges

1. Preheat the oven to 400°F (200°C). Wash the sweet potatoes and carefully slice them into wedges.

2. Place the wedges in an large baking sheet and brush olive oil over them. Roast them for 25 minutes, or until lightly browned.

Battered fish

To test the oil is hot enough, an adult can drop in a small piece of bread. If it sizzles, it's ready!

1. Put the flour, baking soda, paprika, and soda water in a mixing bowl, season with black pepper, then whisk until smooth.

2. Ask an adult to heat the sunflower oil in a deep-sided frying pan until it reaches 375°F (190°C). Coat the fish in the batter.

3. Ask an adult to cook the fish until it's golden brown. Remove the fish with a slotted spoon. Drain on paper towels.

Why does batter puff up when it's cooked?
Soda water and baking soda are added to the batter mixture to provide air bubbles. This process is called "aeration." When the batter is fried it puffs up because of the air that's trapped in the mixture, which expands when heated.

Marinated lime chicken

The zingy lime and fresh cilantro leaves give this dish a delicious combination of refreshing flavors. Serve with potatoes and your choice of vegetables.

You will need:

 80 mins   30 mins   4

For the marinade:

• juice of 4 limes, plus 1 lime, finely sliced
• handful of cilantro, finely chopped
• 2 garlic cloves, peeled and finely sliced

Other ingredients:

• 4 skinless chicken breasts
• 2 eggs
• 3 cups bread crumbs
• 4 tbsp sunflower oil, for frying (1 tbsp per chicken breast)
• potatoes and beans, to serve

① Carefully make four small cuts on the top of each chicken breast to help marinate flavor into the meat.

② Make the marinade by mixing all the ingredients in a bowl. Place the chicken in the marinade. Cover the bowl with plastic wrap and chill for one hour in the refrigerator.

③ Beat the eggs in a bowl and place one piece of chicken in the bowl. Turn the chicken breast so it gets covered in egg.

④ Coat the chicken breast in bread crumbs. Repeat steps 3 and 4 for each piece of chicken. Discard any remaining marinade.

⑤ Fry the chicken in oil over medium heat for 10-15 minutes on each side. The chicken needs to be cooked through, with no sign of pink.

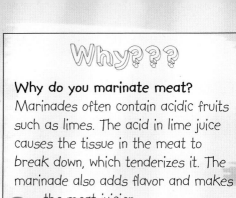

Why???

Why do you marinate meat?
Marinades often contain acidic fruits such as limes. The acid in lime juice causes the tissue in the meat to break down, which tenderizes it. The marinade also adds flavor and makes the meat juicier.

Muffins make a delicious dessert. The blueberries make the muffins extra moist and yummy. They pop while they cook, adding great bursts of color.

You will need:

 15 mins   20 mins   12

- 3½ tbsp unsalted butter
- 2¼ cups self-rising flour
- 1 tsp baking powder
- 5 tbsp superfine sugar
- finely grated zest of 1 lemon (optional)
- 1 cup plain yogurt
- 2 large eggs, lightly beaten
- 1½ cups blueberries

Special equipment:
- 12-cup muffin pan and paper baking cups

1 Preheat the oven to 400°F (200°C). Line a 12-cup muffin pan with paper baking cups.

2 Melt the butter in a pan; set aside. Sift the flour and baking powder into a bowl; mix in the sugar and zest. Make a well in the center.

3 Mix the yogurt, eggs, and cooled melted butter together in a large pitcher, then pour into the dry ingredients.

4 Add the blueberries. Mix until just combined, but don't overmix, or the muffins will be heavy.

5 Spoon evenly into the baking cups and bake for 20 minutes, or until golden and springy. Cool in the pan for five minutes.

Why???

Why do the muffins rise in the oven? By adding baking powder to all-purpose flour or by using self-rising flour you are adding a rising agent. Baking powder reacts with the other ingredients in the recipe, releasing bubbles of carbon dioxide. When you cook the muffins, the air bubbles get larger and make your muffins rise into a bigger size than when you placed them in the oven.

Extras
Use raspberries in place of
blueberries, or orange zest
instead of the lemon.

Put half the muffins in an
airtight container and place in the
freezer to have at a later date.
The muffins can stay in the
freezer for up to two months.

You will need:

🥣 20 mins 🕐 25 mins 🍴 10

For the cake:
- I cup butter, at room temperature
- I cup superfine sugar
- 4 large eggs, lightly beaten
- 2 cups self-rising flour
- confectioners' sugar, to dust

For the filling:
- ½ cup heavy cream
- 6oz (175g) strawberries, hulled and sliced

Special equipment:
- 2 x 8in (20cm) shallow cake pans
- electric hand mixer
- parchment paper

Make this delicious cake for a family party or for a friend's birthday. You'll have lots of fun filling it with strawberries and decorating it with confectioners' sugar.

1) Ask an adult to preheat the oven to 350°F (180°C). Line the pans with parchment paper. ⚠

2) Mix the butter and sugar with an electric hand mixer until light and creamy. Beat in the eggs a little at a time.

3) Sift in the flour and fold it in gently with a metal spoon.

4) Divide the mixture between the pans and bake for 25 minutes. Cool briefly in the pans, then turn onto a wire rack to cool.

5) Beat the cream in a bowl. Put the strawberries and cream on one cake. Place the other cake on top. Dust thickly with confectioners' sugar.

Extras

When strawberries aren't in season (or if you want something different), try using 6oz (175g) of peaches or apricots from a can. Make sure you drain the peaches or apricots from the juices that they are preserved in.

Fruity meringues

You will need:

  30 mins · 90 mins · 6

- 3 large egg whites
- 11 tbsp superfine sugar
- ½ cup confectioners' sugar
- ½ tsp ground cinnamon
- 18oz (500g) package mixed frozen berries, defrosted
- grated zest of 1 orange
- 1¼ cups heavy cream or whipping cream

Special equipment:
- electric hand mixer
- parchment paper

For a special treat make this tower of meringues and fruit. It's a perfect dessert for a party. Invite a group of your friends over to help you make and eat this dish!

1 Ask an adult to preheat the oven to 250°F (130°C). Line a baking sheet with parchment paper.

2 Beat the egg whites until stiff peaks form. Beat in 7 tbsp of the superfine sugar a tablespoonful at a time, until stiff.

3 Sift in the confectioners' sugar, and half a teaspoon of cinnamon, and fold them in with a large spoon.

4 Spoon the mixture onto the baking tray in six heaps. Cook for 1½ hours (until crisp). Leave to cool on a wire rack for 30 minutes.

5 Put the frozen berries in a pan with the orange zest and the remaining sugar and cook for one minute, or until the juice runs.

Why???

Why do the egg whites become stiff when you beat them? Egg whites are made up of water and proteins. The proteins are really delicate and when they're beaten they get tangled up. This traps air and forms a stiff white foam— perfect for making meringues. Make sure there isn't any egg yolk or grease in the bowl when you beat the egg whites, otherwise it won't work.

6) Put the cream in a mixing bowl and beat with an electric hand mixer until soft peaks form. Make a tower of meringues, cream, and fruit.

Put any leftover pieces of meringue in an airtight container. Use within three days.

Lemon and lime cake

The lemon and lime juice make this cake scrumptiously moist and full of flavor. The runny glaze icing adds an extra sweetness. Share it with your family and friends.

You will need:

 15 mins  60 mins 12

- ¾ cup butter, at room temperature
- ¾ cup superfine sugar
- 3 large eggs, lightly beaten
- grated zest of 1 lemon
- grated zest of 1 lime
- 2 tbsp lemon juice
- 1½ cups self-rising flour
- 2 tbsp poppy seeds (optional)
- 1 tbsp lime juice
- ⅔ cup confectioners' sugar

Special equipment:
- electric hand mixer

1 Ask an adult to preheat the oven to 350°F (180°C).

2 Using an electric hand mixer, mix in the butter and superfine sugar until light and fluffy. Line a loaf pan with baking parchment.

3 Beat in the eggs a little at a time, then gently fold in the lemon and lime zest, together with one tablespoon of the lemon juice. Sift in the flour, then fold in with the poppy seeds, if using.

4 Transfer to the pan and smooth the top. Bake for one hour, or until golden. Cool in the pan for five minutes, then move to a wire rack.

5 Mix the remaining lemon juice with the lime juice. Sift in the confectioners' sugar; combine to make a runny icing. Spoon it over the cake.

Why???

Why is confectioners' sugar so fine? Confectioners' sugar is a lot finer than granulated sugar because it has been ground to a powder. That's why it's also called powdered sugar. You aren't able see the sugar crystals in it, since it's so fine. It dissolves very easily in liquid, which is why it's used for icings on cakes, cookies, and pastries.

Ice cream

Pour, mix, and shake your way through this recipe to make a delicious and refreshing ice cream. This frozen dessert doesn't have to go in the freezer!

You will need:

 12 mins

- ½ tbsp sugar
- ½ cup milk
- ½ cup heavy cream
- ¼ tsp vanilla extract
- 2lb (900g) ice cubes
- ½ cup coarse salt
- mixed berries (optional)

Special equipment:
- 2 resealable bags, 1 bigger than the other

(1) Whisk the sugar, milk, heavy cream, and vanilla in a bowl. Pour the mixture into a resealable bag, close it, and set aside.

(2) Put the ice cubes into a large bowl and pour the coarse salt over the ice.

Keep your hands on the towel so they don't freeze!

(3) Fill a large resealable bag halfway with ice cubes. Place the sealed bag of cream mixture into the bag of ice.

(4) Fill up the rest of the large bag with ice cubes and close it.

(5) Wrap the large bag in a dish towel and shake for 10 minutes, or until the cream mixture has become a solid. Serve immediately.

Why do you add the salt to the ice? Because dissolving the salt absorbs energy from the ice-water mix. This lowers the temperature of the liquid to below the melting point of ice, creating an environment in which the cream mixture can freeze.

You can also serve your ice cream with chocolate sauce or pieces.

Raspberry crème brûlée

This traditional French dessert is fun to make and eat. Crème brûlée means "burnt cream" and it gets its name from the burnt (caramelized) sugar on top.

You will need:

 10 mins   30 mins   6

- 7oz (200g) fresh raspberries
- 4 large egg yolks
- 5 tbsp golden superfine sugar
- 2¼ cups heavy cream
- 1 tsp vanilla extract

Special equipment:
- 6 ramekins
- electric hand mixer

1) Divide the raspberries among the ramekins. Beat the egg yolks and two tablespoons of sugar in a bowl until pale and creamy.

2) Heat the cream gently (don't boil) for five minutes. Remove from the heat, stir in the vanilla, and allow to cool for five minutes.

3) Slowly add the warm cream to the egg mixture, beating constantly. Pour the mixture back into the pan, and cook over low heat (do not boil) for a couple of minutes, stirring constantly. If overheated, the custard will curdle.

Be careful when pouring the warm custard.

Why???

Why does the sugar get hard and brown? When the crème brûlées are heated under a broiler, the sugar on top gets hard and brown because the sugar melts and caramelizes, giving it a delicious nutty flavor. This process is called "pyrolysis."

4) Pour the custard into the ramekins and allow to cool. Transfer to the refrigerator to set for a couple of hours.

5) Sprinkle the custards evenly with the remaining sugar. Place under a hot broiler until the sugar bubbles and browns.

Allow the topping to harden for 20 minutes *before* serving.

Refrigerator cake

Try out this delicious chocolate treat. It makes quite a few pieces, so you can freeze half of them in an airtight container and use within three months.

You will need:

 10 mins   2 mins   (24)

- 1lb (450g) graham crackers
- 11 tbsp butter
- 9oz (250g) dark chocolate, broken into pieces
- 2 tbsp light corn syrup
- ⅓ cup raisins
- ½ cup almonds, roughly chopped

Special equipment:
- 7x7in (18x18cm) pan
- parchment paper

1 Place the graham crackers in a plastic bag and crush them with a rolling pin. Don't break them too finely though.

2 Stir the butter, chocolate, and syrup in a bowl over a pan of hot water, until melted. Remove the pan and bowl from the heat.

Don't forget to line your pan with parchment paper.

Why???

Why do you line the pan with parchment paper instead of aluminum foil? Parchment paper is covered in a nonstick coating so it stops the food from sticking to the pan.

Why do you chill the refrigerator cake? You chill the chocolate cake to make it set. The cool temperature of the refrigerator brings down the temperature of the melted chocolate, making it turn into a solid again.

3 Stir in the crackers, raisins, and almonds. Make sure all the ingredients are mixed well.

4 Use a masher to press the mixture into a pan that is lined with parchment paper. Put in the refrigerator to harden.

Index

Cakes
  lemon and lime cake 56–57
  refrigerator cake 62–63
  strawberry cake 52–53
Cookies
  apricots and cinnamon 22–23
  Cheddar cheese and rosemary 22–23
  cocoa and white chocolate 22–23
  Parmesan and pumpkin seed 22–23
  pesto, tomato, and olive 22–23
  raisin spice 22–23
  tomato paste and pine nuts 22–23
  traditional chocolate chip 22–23
Crème brûlée 60–61
Crêpes 10

Dough
  cookie 22–23
  pizza 32–33, 34, 35

Eggs
  boiled 9
  French toast 12–13
  fried 9
  scrambled 8

Fish
  cod 46
  pollock 46
  shrimp skewers 24–25
  tuna and bean salad 31

Granola 14–15, 16–17

Hummus
  olive 28
  sun-dried tomato 28

Ice cream 58–59

Meat dishes
  chili con carne 44–45
  ham and pineapple pizza 35
  lamb hot pot 38–39
  marinated lime chicken 48–49
  mini-burgers 40–41
  pea and mint soup with bacon 20
  pepper and pepperoni pizza 35
  scrambled eggs with bacon 8
Moussaka
  meat and eggplant 37
  vegetarian 36–37
Muffins
  blueberry 50–51

Pancakes 10–11
Pasta
  pasta with beef and mushroom sauce 43
  pasta with no-cook tomato sauce 42
Pizza
  ham and pineapple pizza 35
  mozzarella and mushroom pizza 34, 35
  pepper and pepperoni pizza 35
  tomato and olive pizza 35
Popcorn
  savory popcorn 29
  sweet popcorn 29

Potatoes
  sweet potato wedges 46–47

Rice
  rice balls 26–27
  rice and chili con carne 44

Salads
  dressing 31
  tomato and couscous salad 30
  tuna and bean salad 31
Skewers
  shrimp 24–25
Smoothies
  banana and mango smoothie 19
  blueberry, orange, and strawberry smoothie 18
  peach and berry smoothie 19
Soup
  pea and mint 20–21

Techniques
  basting 24
  beating 22, 52, 53, 54, 55, 56
  bread crumbs, making 26, 40
  broiling 8
  cake pan, lining 52, 56, 62
  folding in 56
  kneading 32, 33
  marinating 24, 48–49
  sifting 32, 52, 56
  whisking 8, 10, 12, 46, 58, 60

There are so many fun dishes to try out!

Acknowledgments

Dorling Kindersley would like to thank the children who appeared in the photographs: Roberto Barney Allen, Fiona Lock, Peter Lock, Serena Patel, Christian Rivas-Lastic, Eva Rose Menzie, Ella Menzie, Omid Alavi, George Arnold, and Alexander Whillock.

We would also like to thank Jan Stevens for recipe testing, Lisa Linder for photography, Jennifer Lane for proofreading, Jennifer Murray and Marc Staples for production editorial assistance, and Alexander Cox for editorial work on this book.